A Part of the Main

LESLEY SAUNDERS | PHILIP GROSS

A CONVERSATION

MULFRAN PRESS

A Part of the Main is a single poem by two poets who conducted a dialogue in verse by email over the course of a few months. Born of the difficult feelings and public discord arising from the events of 2016, it moves deeper into the cultural hoard of the British Isles in search of a humane understanding of migration and identity.

A Part of the Main

'*we work with the longing for lost texts to be discovered, for every broken thing to be repaired…*'   Edmund Richardson

... an old story
      told over and again
of an island
      full of time and dusk
a figure
      half-inhabiting the shore
heart-break
      ruining her quick eyes
a far mist
      mimicking a ship's sail
there
      then not there...

ah but who
      could be framing
this scape, whose
      eyes (between
the shrubbery)
      see mist-mirage
and equally
      her lengthening
half-self, thinning
      shadow on the sand,
who but yours truly,
      my dear: Caliban?

oh yes, these isles have need
of their moon-calf,
a broken voice
to bell their hurts,
one who dreams
of swales and straits,
mains and deeps
of clear blue water,
lullaby sounds
of the shipping news,
those sweet airs
that make him cry.
his eyes are oceans,
big with storm.

ah, gerrroff with you
      as my old Mam said.
you sound like His books.
      good kindling, mind,
nights when I'm hearth-
      sick and have two
dry twigs to rub together.
      (douse the smoke
come morning. some good soul
      might get it in his head
to stage a rescue.
      where would we be then?)

... come morning
    and she's the one
going off in a huff
    of haar, hers the face
in the sail
    and not a word spoken,
the swell all glitter
    and foam, the life-boat
adrift and turning
    its back to the smoke
on the shore:
    wine-dark it's not,
the *mare* that's
    nostrum, all ours,
fog-patched,
    doggered, pill-boxed,
on the brink,
    in the offing, the drink.
is she the one waving?

or… who are these
shipwrecks-in-waiting
in the sea lanes, crowding
to the gunwhales? steady it,
the *kylix*, elegant
but cracked, too wide
and slopping storm-wine
and green-queasy
water to and fro.
from continent to continent.
where are there islands
or a lingua franca
generous enough to entertain
the thought of them, of
us, in leaky life-vests,
one hand waving from
a porthole, cargo in the hold?

(Aferdita displaced
     from Fushë Kosovë,
Hecuba and Fatmeh
     from Troy aka Homs,
Effie from Aulis,
     Dido from Tunis,
Mirjana who has seen
     the Virgin Mary,
Minditsi, Ostelinda,
     Tematea, Zujenia
from the Black Sea
     via Romani roads,
Antigone from nation,
     brothers, past, future,
Fadwa running shoeless
     over broken glass,
all of them,
     clinging to each other
and their black bin-bag
     of cook-pans
down history's
     teeming waterways
and out on a raft
     into the roar
and wave-mass
     polyphloisboio thalassēs)

dried petals, papery,
      a homecoming garland
or wreath in the shrine
      on the cliff. Our Lady.
for your mercy. oh,
      Aphrodite, oh Asherah, Star
of the Sea. the coastguard
      boat is out again
hauling them in. still
      the beaches are strewn
with bodies in their sun oil,
      the shipwreck of plenty.
we the people of the mirage
      look up. have these others
come to wake us from our dream?

Caliban cliff-faced
     and wind-shaven
shape-shifts,
     makes for the open.
sheds his skins
     as he dives like a stone
through the ooze
     till he seems to see
a body or shoal
     with no borders
or cordons –
     his cold
his innermost vast.
     at first no words come
just fish-scales of light
     that glimmer and play
in the inky abyss.
     then drowned shapes
reach out to him,
     the lost verbs inscribed
in *me   you   us*
     deep shades of meaning
that eeled their way
     westward through Europe
from the Pontos Euxeinos
     (hospitable sea)
to now and here…

mare internum: close
your eyes, you'll find a whole
        Phoenician sea-truck
down there in the silt,
        its shed load, spilled
amphorae like the stalest stag-do,
        tin from the Cassiterides,
not to mention routine freights
        of beauty – bronze ephebes
lolled among the lobsters. Ariadne
        on her broken *kratēr*,
black-on-red-ware silhouette,
        is the fragment she is. the low
sea-ceiling, though, is overcast
        with slicks, with run-offs
from tired fields, the spill zone
        widening from deltas
of the here and now. oh
        wash us, wash us clean,
they pray: Po, Ebro, Rhone...

... across the Manche
    the sleeve or minch
the moat or trench
    by which the Continent
is conjoined with Kent
    (our foremothers
slipping dryshod
    from Shepway
to the Pas de Calais
    with creels of goby
trod pathways
    through its peat)
we wait for news
    from Paris, Munich,
Nice. (the land
    lay too low, the sea
rose and drowned
    their hunting-grounds.
a harpoon was found,
    antler-tools, a human skull.)
three were Turkish,
    three from Kosovo,
one Greek, a mall
    and promenade knee-deep
in carnations.

lowest tide, and a causeway
of shoals, a wading path
          between bare islands and a sight,
maybe a mirage, of a further shore
          enticed them. no, not *them* –
those out-of-African chancers,
          beach-bums, scavengers,
were *us*, just ask the mother-line,
          your mitochondrial DNA.
now and again the world shifts
          on its axis. tips a spill
from the edge of a continent
          into the sea. the tide-chafe
rising… there is nothing clean
          about floodwater: grief in it,
under-swirls of anger, children's
          cries – can we come home now
mother? – that may be our own.

        … oh Mam, *maman, nënë,*
where are you? Miranda
       yells out in her sleep
as the world keels over
       and the tide spills its waifs
on the shingle.
       can a whole species of feeling
die out like the moths,
       like the lingos Brythonic,
Bargy, or Norn,
       those rare speckled
beauties? visitants
       arriving from over the water,
favouring sweetness
       more even than light,
they were high summer
       once – must the island
mislay yet another
       mud-flat or sand-spit,
one more habitat
       for charity, mercy, grace
(old-fangled names
       for love of the other,
the stranger, the twin)?

we are not brave,
nor this new world that seems…
that seems to…
(let's leave it at that:
'that seems'). the Caliban
amongst us, in us,
writhes
in his cramps, his breath
stitched up in him;
he's a thicket of thorns,
of voices scolding, whips
of brambles: thou dost not know
thine own meaning.
and when Ariel drops in
to share some rare find
for his butterfly collection,
small wonder there's a spitting
in the wind. fuck charity.
it hurts. the language
hurts. is hurt.   we hurt…
together? no, against
each other.   it's a bloody
tempest out there.
how are we supposed to sing?

       … impasse, then? not a
Prospero in sight while
      the seas under your sullen
skies run snotgreen
      and of the coral-reefs
bare bones are made.
      look at yourselves –
a jumble of rocks,
      an empire of thin air…
what's new or brave,
      where's your magic,
your mutinous art? drown
      your grief in booze,
boil your brains,
      sleep through it all.
or go sing to the sea
      thalassa ēchēessa –
who knows, it may sing back…

old Gogmagog lies crumpled
on the beach, like the buckle-kneed
       girders of the rusting pier.
old gun-emplacements, rather –
       the sinking East coast
of this skew-whiff island
       wears them jauntily
until the final slither. ah
       well, let the old dog
off the lead, watch him lolloping
       down to the tide line,
barking at the crash, recoiling,
       and barking again.
we hardly see
       that the horizon's faded,
sea mist rising, until
       a faint whickering chink
of rigging says: look up
       – white sails in the mist,
and voices, too close,
       small and flinty clear,
the way mist does.
       this is another border.
we are not quite anywhere.

   – or everywhere and nowhere,
King Lud's kingdom
   of castaways and chantymen
our call and response
   containing more rhyme
than reason, heave and haul,
   the push and pull of a chorus
not quite or yet in synch
   and hoarse against the wind
can't you hear the gulls a-callin'?
   this chanting or cantering
the length of the fetch –
   wilt come? I'll follow.

if there's a rhythm in this
    it's the heave-ho of the sea
against the ship's flank,
    a shudder and crack
when it catches you broadside.
    and likewise its swing and its smack
against the cliff. we need it.
    the Matter of Britain is foam-fringed.
so we are enchanted.
    here's Brutus, coming bruised
from Troy, here's Tristan and Iseult
    all at sea, here's a land
weighed down with sleeping giants.
    thud, thud – the Atlantic
like a drunken porter at the gate.
    King Lud, if anything
can stir him, might awake
    as Ned Ludd, loom-breaker
ripping the threads of a fate
    in which he could not find himself,
his heart or his hand.
    transport him. once more,
let the sea take care of this.

some things it will not swallow
– bits of life-vest, pelagic plastics
gyring in the wide Sargasso
that'll come back to bite us
like moon-struck women
we've grown ashamed of,
call by names not their own,
abuse, betray.
her head is full of elvers,
tiny spectres of light
flexing their way
through a limpid landless blue
to the hungry river-mouths
of England and the dreary
peep of Kentish plovers.
ghost-ship now, she spills
herself on the breakers,
corpo santo, butterfly's-wing.

four thousand metres deep
　　　　the submersible's single-
minded stare catches this
　　　　in its eye-beam: a rippling
frisson of its near-transparent
　　　　almost nothingness,
a polychaete worm
　　　　self-wafted on the shiver
of its frills – not so much that
　　　　it knows where it is going as
its going knows it, knows
　　　　the way the world of water
knows and breathes itself
　　　　around the calloused,
frontier-fissured crusts,
　　　　scar tissue, old wounds,
we call land. one rainy night
　　　　the fields are glistening
all across the Levels
　　　　pouring westwards
as the eels remember
　　　　something we've forgotten,
abandon their ditches
　　　　and make for the sea.

what country *is* this? hard to tell
       beneath the scorched earth
and waterlog – fens and levels
       that are not quite dry land,
where wetness looks after things
       we'd rather forget, bog bodies
with slit throats, bronze blades
       nicked and burred with violent use,
half-eaten food tipped over
       and flung aside in the chaos
of a night-time raid, a bracelet
       of blue glass beads unstrung.
wall-carpets lie in the mud
       along with their loom-weights,
pictures that have been pinned
       to the fence for too many years,
brothers', cousins' faces faded
       past recognition. we needed
a safe house in those days,
       somewhere over the water
until rain silenced the fires.

        ... as if water was our friend.
(she seemed to be,
        bringer of those tiny crafted
skies or eyes of glass across
        a continent, from the heart
of the world – threading intricate
        coastlines, traded hand to hand,
inlet to inlet, to here.)
        we should have listened
to the whisper-hush of reeds
        and guessed how what we laid
in fermentation, layer by layer,
        on the mere-bed, would rise
as Grendel, crudely hewn
        like the roots of the language
dripping blood, marsh-mud,
        alliteration... roaring somewhat
before toppling back maimed
        and whimpering for cool,
for smell of reed stalks
        retting in dark water,
and for mother.   mother,
        take the pain I am away.

when the weather breaks,
      he's still there, Caliban, Kyklops,
hutched in a wilderness
      of longing, backed against
the cliff-edge, hurting
      and homesick in his homeland.
head down he combs
      the stones for the unrhymed
missing bits of his story,
      for a world that fits his words,
but cannot find a version
      of himself that unmakes
the monster that he is –
      āglæca, fiendish and greedy
for soulfood, he'll be guest
      at the hero-host's feast,
like the bee-wolf
      he's loped from an otherwhere
into the heart of our village,
      a kenning sung by a gleeman,
a pedlar's fylfot, a spell.

what salve for his soul
could the sea bring – the pitiless
        Norse, or else the memory
we are already exiles. Heorot
        after all is elsewhere. the dark
mere, like our own estrangement,
        followed, shadow in the water
underneath our keel. the Cymric
        caught it at our touch.
pass it on. the Matter of Europe
        is not being written, not yet,
except as the Latin of Rome
        turns to dust of itself,
its priests dressed like the absences
        of men. if I trust a monk
it's one who stands up to his chin
        in icy water, bawling his psalms
at the sea, who leaves space
        in the thicket of words for beard
or beast to peek through,
        who edges his book
with garnet and amethyst,
        beach-scrabbled stones,
the glint of north light in them.

       pass the torch from hand to hand
as *aglaos*, dark-shining –
       a bushel of beeswax candles, or
a dozen unlit beacon-fires
       built on black-mountain hillforts
waiting for the Romans,
       French, English, Spanish, Danes
to show their faces,
       soldier-husbands who stayed
or left: the rough wooing
       of our European lineage.
(Dido hugs his shirt
       to smell again the smell of him
dulces exuviae
       the mess of their bed-clothes
like a creature they'd made
       in the cave of their nights.
her pyre is voluptuous
       with smoke, a sweet citrussy
choke as close as the glair
       or glare of his absence, *aglaos*.)
we do not dream in esperanto.

skriking, scrabbling for air
like a man in a shipwreck –
     he was never more a stranger,
Mother said, than then
     when he drowned in those dreams,
all Europe choked up in him,
     a curse in German, or in Russian,
at each other's throats and
     his, and lodged there… later
as he came to gasping
     on the shingle of their bed
she could not say which
     of them, he with that ruined
continent inside him, or
     she out on this raw edge
of the west, was offshore, truly
     cast off, cast away.

here's where it all comes together
        or apart, among roots we can't see,
the dark tree standing behind
        the house in the photograph
where people are shading
        their eyes so we're not sure
if that's Joe or John with his arm
        around Mother and whether
the war had already begun,
        which would explain the frocks
though not the border of crocuses
        over there at the edge,
fresh votive offerings, bodies
        turned by the gods into flickers
of cobalt and chrome
        that the Kodak can't quite catch.

should the dead have a vote?
      the evidence of history suggests
some do. here they come,
      still blinking from a whole
mappa mundi and more
      of afterwheres: the burning longship
drifting back inshore, smeech
      gathering back to body,
hurt and old... the plague pit,
      tinkers, drabs and hucksters
back at it already bartering
      their bones, on the thin ice of life
like a frost fair... the shuffling
      wisps down corridors of sanitoria,
the commonillhealth of the sick
      the length of Europe, endless spas
as if the waters really cared...
      the unnamed, always, at the roadside,
this march, that construction project
      in the swamp, their rags and flags
mud-coloured... and the children,
      all those children. this will take
some time, the counting.
      when we have the numbers
we'll know what to do.

some of our realities are plural,
spectacles, clothes, genitals,
    measles, hearts & minds, days
of wine & roses, bearings,
    just deserts. others are only
singular – milk, dust, fry,
    furniture, knowledge, wealth.
how do we count what counts?
    by watching our language, minding
our tongue, a matter of getting
    our minds and hearts around
and past the herd, the mob,
    the swarm coming in on the tide
(that river of blood)? Or by
    the body's own idioms, solace
of hands in the mud and soot
    between the alarms and excursions,
a collective of nouns like syn-pathos,
    con-cordia, con-scientia,
diesen Kuß der ganzen Welt, networks
    of rhizomes under the wire?

the weighing of the heart
          proceeds in Aisle K. please
wait patiently. a baby snuffles
          at the breast, under indigo
folds, its own night, safe
          here as in any desert. hoosh
back that toddler ducked under the tape
          out of line, his grin
escaping. we will need to see
          some evidence. is there anything
here that in the wrong hands
          could convict you? a shuddering
grips us, in the long shed,
          as another flight strains
at its traces, tethered thunder.
          these impartial angels. later
you will see your bag, your purse,
          outlined in night sight grey,
its archaeology of hair grip,
          spiral binding, amulet,
and step into the – stop
          there, arms up – portal.
on the screen, papery walls
          of a heart lapse and grip
around their unknowable contents.
          did you let anybody
pack your bags for you?

say goodbye to your loved ones,
this is the end of the road for you.
        Tomis – twinned with Rome it ain't,
where the Danube empties itself
        into the Sea of shipwrecks and gas-
seeps, beluga and plankton-bloom.
        he imagines driving solo, non-stop
through Thracia, Illyria, Dalmatia,
        car boot chinking with a dozen litres
of cheap Primitivo wine, then on into
        Pannonia with its coastline of chalets
and pines before being stopped
        at the border. Italy. he's crossed
a line somewhere, won't be let
        home. not ever. poet of sex
and metamorphosis, his terrible *error*
        was *amor*, Rome's mirror-image.
 now he must learn to spell exile
        in verse, traffic in metrical pathos,
speak Scythian-Greek to make
        himself heard over the wind.
writing a poem that won't, will
        never, be read is like doing a dance
on your own in the dark.

                    the wrong sea, one you face across
away from wherever, in a world
          of surging overlapping Tristia,
we'll call Rome. rant at it if you will
          with your mouth full of pebbles
that used to be words, the names
          you wake calling at night, too,
swallowed by its white noise
          in your head. (Pontos Euxeinos
was publicist's spin, shameless
          as 'Greenland'.) but the wrong
sea makes its inroads anywhere
          and way inland – not just
the tideline turned out daily
          by the hostels on the Newport Road,
without leave to go or remain,
          but whole estates
wake up, born here, to airwaves full
          of blandishment, words, words
that only seem to be their own,
          and feel the wrong sea lapping
round them, and want… how
          to say it? somewhere
to go back to. somebody to blame.

      meaning's strained to break-
point, the words migrate,
      hoik sense from its moorings,
truthfulness from its roots
      in syntax, that basic link
between logic and language
      – which in Syntagma Square
under icy-clear skies seemed
      straightforward enough,
no more on the one hand
      and on the other, these people
eating scraps out of dustbins,
      those always setting the rules.
elpida erchetai, there'd be
      holidays and hospitals for all,
clothes on the children's backs,
      red carnations for the street-singers,
free cocktails of hope
      and rebetiko. look it up
in your musty old primer
      – austerity's the word for
wine's dryness, all its sugars
      fully fermented. then read
and remember: *the Greeks*
      are not willing to obey those
they consider barbarians.

it's us, not just words, who find
ourselves shipwrecked a little
in translation, all the languages
we are: we who pitch the verb
in early… we who set out all
our pieces on the board before we move?
the constant soundproofed mutter
behind glass of the translators
in their word hive, that's time
spooling forwards or back
through earphones, the dry chittering
of wings. what comes through
is language in a kind of afterlife,
the dullest waiting room of heaven.
who wouldn't be caught now and then
doodling Xs in the margin?
'exit' being Latin, needs no gloss,
and being theatre, and this being the sea
coast of Bohemia, well,
who isn't waiting for the bear?

out beyond the harbour
the heartwrecks loom
            through the murk, heads
turned to stone by silt
            and tide. such sadness
in their lidless eyes,
            the diver in her anti-fogging mask
has to blink the tears away.
            or so I like to think. in the sea
off Syracuse another cargo
            wine oil salt blossom-honey slaves
washed away, no trace left
            of those golden-age goods.
only the corals sprouting
            from their once-fingertips
remember (do they?)
            the cold lingering touch
of the sea-goddess,
            quicksilver flick of tiny fish,
the endless gift-exchange
            down beyond the light-zone.
whoever is called on by name
            Poseidon Adonai Allah Aphrodite
on the lips of the drowning
            dive now on the steely lifeline
of your inheld breath
            to them, the newborn dead,
living reef, sunken treasure.
            move heaven and earth.

nowhere better than this
> to convene – in the silt.
draw back the grey silk curtains,
> stirred up again, as if
the mud from the centuries' trenches
> was slipping from gravity's grip.
was sublimating into mist.
> where better than the dream
of all Atlantises, from Santorini's
> chewed rind (a stunned cruise ship
tiny in its crater) to lost Lyonesse?
> (I've seen the stone row wading
out and underwater. I was holidaying
> on the Cassiterides.) no heroes
better than these, the eyeless,
> limbless, sunk, without rank,
names or papers. if *l'Homme Armé*
> comes home from the Crusades
keep him well caged inside
> the leaps and fountain-fall
of Josquin's music. if you have treaties
> to sign, sign them here.

did we sail as far as Thule
        that extraordinary summer?
the shell-sound of the ocean,
        its call like a gasping for air
dis, quand reviendras-tu?
        strung above the land's anglosaxon –
or was it the piping of a fife
        in time to boots and tattoos
(Arthur's boys in grizzled blankets,
        the matter of Britain a drawn sword
dipped in vermilion, goldleaved)
        we really wanted to believe
we could hear? trace back
        our ancestors to oak and ash,
in our mind's ears not *chanson*
        or *saga* tuned to the blast-horn
but a faint waft of plainsong
        snagged on the gale-facing scarps
of archipelago, shoeless lament
        for a maimed king? I remember,
do you, it was well past midnight
        and we were still sitting there
insubstantial as woodsmoke
        watching the sea turn to fire.
was it then we saw them
        wading drenched and naked
out of the sea, mantling
        themselves in the gold-foil sheets
as if they were regal robes,
        waving the plastic water-bottles
like conductors' wands,
        then breaking into song?

well, naturally. when you *live*
        facing it, nobody's ocean
but its own, no wonder
        there are... wonders. what couldn't
occur? the saint washed clunking
        up onto a bare strand in a barrel
– no, see how it breeds
        in the telling: he was *born*
between shores, his mother cast off,
        cast out, him already sailing
in the leaky vessel of her.
        and his first cries, to the arctic terns,
his preaching. the crimp of the wave
        at the margin of the words,
however scribed, however holy,
        breeds these curlicues:
leap, salmon, and gape, dragon, such
        illuminations, a whole new world
glimpsed through an uncial O.
        it was not for the soul of a mere nation
that we wrangled with the polished
        delegation sent by Rome.
it was for... what? the sky
        stretched, opened, by the beat
of wild goose wings.
        the west. we ended haggling
around the date of Easter. lost,
        as God intended maybe –
never meant to be the text
        but its torn edge, apart
and a part of it. trying to say that
        we sounded like fools.

– yes: holy fools, unruly folk
        naked to the world's weathers,
given to dreams and devotions
        of noticing, those pipit-eggs
in the undergrowth, these
        feathery *incipits*, still-living words
that gleam like starling-wings,
        weaving nests out of texts.
they call it insular, this art
        that minusculed its way across
the incunabula of small nations,
        burrowing into hairline cracks between.
it was certain of something, of god
        in every creature, of burning visions
in a tree at Peckham Rye,
        of resurrection by the Thames.
(but the breeze always blows on us
        from somewhere else, Scythia
to north-Umbria, Nazareth
        to Cookham, Jerusalem as far as
Primrose Hill.) it never asked,
        is flesh the revelation or a veil,
should we follow the flower
        or hold the line, or just doodle
exquisitely in the margins –
        it knew hereafter as forever here-
and-now. I'd give heart-and-soul,
        the marrow of my geriatric bones,
for that.

the bones of the old
are a sensitive instrument,
        a form of divination. I don't
mean the relics of saints –
        unless that's Saint Caliban,
doing the hobble-dance now,
        joints burning, like his martyred
Ma before him. he's on fire
        with presence, in the body,
wrong 'un though it is.
        some evenings on the clifftop,
he's a wicker man, a wrecker's
        light for the unwary, he's the guy
who climbs the bonfire of himself
        to let out a glorious belch
of smoke, sparks and vituperation.
        the old bugger. don't tell me
that's not a kind of glory,
        even praise. it's not pretty, for sure.
nor are some of the words
        the crowds are chanting, but
it does nail us here, in the heart
        of the times. do we want care?
(we do) in the community? (we
        want one, so much that it
hurts) if we desire to live
        together, then we live with this.

oh him again, crawling out
      from the wormy woodwork,
blind in one eye now
      but grinning through the matt
of his food-stained beard –
      falstaffing all our princely
(and princessly) pretensions,
      sprawling full-length on a bench
like a bed-blocker, his trolley
      of ownings flowing over with junk
like grief, rage, fear, damage,
      despair, the toxic waste we make
believe's not there. and so
      he smells of piss and bargain booze,
slurs his curses *sotto voce*, yes
      he's the body politic all right,
emblem of our corporate realm
      come to make these islands
great again. as you drop
      your small change in his palm
take care not to let him get
      too close, don't try to meet
his one-eyed gaze. and never
      tell him you've seen through
his disguise, you've guessed
      he's Lobby Lud the mystery man
aka the dolorous king, hurt healer,
      the god within.

a world of night-light, night shift,
		gently humming. blue-green
carpet, ripple-patterned,
		in a corridor that looks the same
both ways. it's him, adrift
		again. third time this week,
she is steering his hand
		from the wrong door handle,
him blinking as if with a new gaze
		at her, at here – where… ?
who are you? as she inches him back
		– this way now, Mr C dear,
this is where you live – she knows
		what follows, his: can't understand
a word of it, your monkey gabble,
		where're you from, where's that
when it's at home? on the edge
		of his bed now, he consents
to sit. is still, and won't let go
		her hand. she wonders, but
it's too late now, whether to tell him
		again, about the visa. or
her name. this time tomorrow
		she'll be on a plane, appeal
rejected, case closed, gone.

back to no man's land,
a strand or liminal space
        (the narrowest of gaps
or slips between deep
        water and skyscraper cliff)
where anything ungood
        could happen, a looking-
glass place where girls grow
        up and old before their time,
the brink or verge, the margin,
        farthest edge, ends of earth,
a brim or hem or fringe,
        a skirt or scarf whose seams
fill grain by grain with sand.
        thus one country becomes
another, a daughter turns
        into orphan, a port to a jungle.

a shudder in the earth's crust,
      in the continent's soul… enough
to wake you, like a hand,
      a lover's, urgent, in the dark.
but this is plain daylight. you jolt:
      were you sleeping, a moment before?
nothing's changed – a few leaves
      shaken early from the weary
London Plane, maybe, who's
      counting? only, everything
stands that bit further apart,
      pavement to pavement, shore
to shore. the fault lines, never
      where you are looking, shift.
see the shawled Big Issue seller
      in her usual doorway? no,
you don't, and that daughter of mist,
      the pale one you always meant
to greet, to give a name
      or place? they could be anywhere
across a landmass sundering
      like a glacier's tongue, ice-towers
crumpling into slow spray,
      frost-fog, where blue-dirty bergs
creak, wallowing apart
      but not far, still grindingly close.

the slab that's Africa comes sliding
      across the Aegean, raising waves.
it's raining fishes over Akrotiri,
      a hell of high water, a blurred hill
of mist and rainbow heaved
      up by the quake, one jacaranda
left standing, and rescuers
      working barehanded for days.
they swill around in aftershock –
      here, here was beauty, or here,
in Amatrice, Arquata, an anywhere
      among whose ruined arcades
beautiful long-legged children
      play at being ghosts, their cries
twittering in the eaves
      like late-summer swallows
then swooping down and away
      to the palm-fringed painted river.
how dreadful the dead are,
      standing there on the bank
with outstretched arms
      as they jilt us again and again.

it's almost a ritual, now
    that the world, its cameras,
can cluster round – days
    after hope gave way, one last
child is delivered from the rubble –
    the midwives in hi-viz and hard hats
with arc lights and slow urgency.
    at first, she's limp as a Pietà
in their arms and this will be the icon
    of the rolling headlines. now
she stirs. tell us, we want
    the jutting microphones (of which
we disapprove) to ask, what language
    are they speaking down there,
where you've been; are bull-dancers
    still vaulting their elegant deaths;
are there street gangs of shades
    in the suburbs that Hades neglects;
is there news? when her eyes open
    it could be on Aleppo
or on carpet-bombed Berlin
    or Carthage, levelled,
sowed with salt – the useless
    question on our lips, the same.

it's all been said, the *ubi nunc*,
      the *hwaer cwom*, the melting
snows and tears of last night,
      the dead ladies, the roses.
I was with the Moabites
      and with the Assyrians,
I was in Italy with Aelfwine,
      I was a lake in the plain,
the bull of seven battles,
      and so I sing and tell a tale,
arrange the bones – here come
      the Sea Peoples, with flood
and famine at their backs,
      we are all descendants of Troy,
when we know what we know
      we will melt away into the trees.
till then, we work with fragments,
      our horse-[chariots?] built from
fig-wood [?], painted crimson.

the motorcades ghost into town,
the more black-and-chrome,
        the more silently attended
by bone-girdered men
        in suits, eyes going everywhere
at once behind their shades,
        the more the powers of the earth
are amongst us… the more bog-pool-
        dark the windows (broken blade
or gold torque spiralling
        into the underworld's fist)…
where was I? this is now,
        these, delegations to the talks
about talks the steel gates
        swing shut on, and it's not
the statements (spit-crackle
        of shutter and flashbulb), it's
the [ ] behind them in the back rooms,
        deal brokered, an [   ]
for a [   ], and down that crack
        a life, a small nation, might slip.
these are the scribes and scholars
        of expedience, the text
we live in, the tablets of clay
        the archaeologists will tease
out gently from beneath
        the broken lintels of the House
of [   ], his [?] royal treasury.

and when they turn our leaves
with their white-gloved fingertips,
or inspect the worn metal moons
of our faces, when they huff
the scurf off our bones, buff up
our eternity rings, what will
the experts conclude? will they
daydream of all our unpaired
cufflinks, broken promises,
the *opus anglicanum*
forgotten, eaten by moth.
or will they tell one another
that we were the lucky ones.
that it was already too late,
though not, yet, the end
of the world. that the ice
had melted while we were infatuated
with gadgets, that the portals
of our community were padlocked
against time, that the hairline
crack, that the crackle of voices
in tongues we didn't speak, that
the seasons, that the oak trees,
the fish-eagle and salmon, that
Saxon and Saami and Gàidhlig,
that the tansy beetle and shrill
carder bee. that our birthright
was not to be great but be kind.

a small boy in a sailor suit
runs at the sea. the gulls
      rise, chiding, on the gust of him.
he is a brief and negligible storm
      they sheer off, spiral up
to join the wind. way down
      he's waving like a castaway,
like Mayday, *m'aidez,* at the sky
      a single line of contrail scores
or *Mama, Papa…* they're a century
      away, his toy empire, further.
we're all on the beach again
      where we began, and every way
we turn it seems an island.
      was that what we wanted?
if by chance a shredded sail
      appears, who'll be the rescued, who
the rescuer? you're wading out,
      the other stumbling in the surf-
scrum shoreward; you open your mouth,
      not knowing whether, if the words
come out, they'll be in language
      understood by anyone
still living.   or any language at all.

Published 2018 by Mulfran Press
2 Aber Street, Cardiff CF11 7AG, UK
www.mulfran.co.uk

printed by Dalton Printers, Cardiff on Parchmarque 90gsm,
cover on Parchmarque 250gsm, with text in Gill Sans Light
and ITC Novarese Book Pro, display in Trajan Pro

ISBN 978-1-907327-31-5

THE
POCKET

DEEP
SLEEP

Published in 2024
by Gemini Adult Books Ltd
Part of Gemini Books Group

Based in Woodbridge and London

Marine House, Tide Mill Way
Woodbridge, Suffolk IP12 1AP
United Kingdom
www.geminibooks.com

Text and Design © 2024 Gemini Books Group
Part of the Gemini Pockets series

Cover image: RGB Ventures/SuperStock/Alamy Stock Photo

ISBN 978-1-80247-266-0

A CIP catalogue record for this book is available from the British Library.

Disclaimer: The book is a guidebook purely for information and entertainment purposes only. All trademarks, individual and company names, brand names, registered names, quotations, celebrity names, logos, dialogues and catchphrases used or cited in this book are the property of their respective owners. The publisher does not assume and hereby disclaims any liability to any party for any loss, damage or disruption caused by errors or omissions, whether such errors or omissions result from negligence, accident or any other cause. This book is an unofficial and unauthorized publication by Gemini Adult Books Ltd and has not been licensed, approved, sponsored or endorsed by any person or entity.

Printed in China

10 9 8 7 6 5 4 3 2 1

Images: Adobe Stock: 18, 35, 76, 77. Shutterstock: 4 Nailotl; 8, 68, 96 yesdoubleyes; 15 Paul Craft; 23 DDDART; 33 frabellins; 36 EVorona; 51 DzmItry; 60, 68, 72, 85, 89, 90, 98, 111, 126 jenny on the moon; 83, 93 novazelandia.

THE POCKET

DEEP SLEEP

Maximize your
most restorative
sleep cycle

CONTENTS

Introduction

We sleep for a third of our lives, and while it was once believed that we shut down while we slumber, we now know that there's a lot going on – though exactly what is still a mystery. Regardless, have a few bad nights' sleep, and it's obvious that sleep is essential for how the body and brain function. Our journey to understanding these night-time hours is like finding a passageway through a maze, but experts are unravelling the science of sleep, including deep sleep. Research is giving us an appreciation for why we sleep, what happens when we don't get enough deep sleep, in particular, and how to improve our chances of getting a good night's rest.

This easy-access book distils the science of sleep into succinct information, advice and tips so that you can boost your mental and physical health through sleep and overcome the obstacles that interfere with your essential rest.

"Sleep is the single most effective thing we can do to reset our brain and body health each day – Mother Nature's best effort yet at contra-death."

Matthew Walker, *Why We Sleep* (2018)

Chapter One

Understanding Sleep

Why do we sleep?

Our ability to live not only relies on us eating and drinking but also on sleeping. When we close our eyes and drift off into sleep, we may not be conscious that our body and brain are still working, however, sleep is an important biological process that is necessary for supporting our brain function and maintaining our physical health.

Rebooting the body

As we sleep, we give our body and brain a chance to "down tools" and rest. Research indicates that we use about 35% less energy when asleep. However, this less-active stage also gives our body an opportunity to repair, maintain and restore various functions, including our:

- heart and circulatory system

- hormones

- metabolism

- respiratory system

- immune system

- memory.

Brain storage

As you sleep, your brain rummages through the events of the day to sort out what memories and useful information are worth storing. It reorganizes nerve cells called neurons and removes any unwanted by-products that build up in the brain during the day. Adequate sleep improves your brain's ability to:

- **learn**

- **memorize**

- **solve problems**

- **be creative**

- **make decisions**

- **focus**

- **concentrate.**

> **Even a soul submerged in sleep is hard at work and helps make something of the world.**

Heraclitus, *Fragments* (c. 500 BCE)

Replenishing energy

While our body is less active during sleep, it can concentrate on resupplying the energy stores that were depleted throughout the day. Our body also uses this time to repair cells and help heal injuries. It explains why an illness such as flu makes us sleepy – your body slows down to focus on fighting off invading viruses and bacteria.

Be aware of how your body feels: if you are recovering from illness, feeling run down, or have had a physically or mentally strenuous day, head to bed and let your body do the work,

Sleep & the heart

Our heart rate and blood pressure drop as we enter non-REM sleep, so our heart doesn't have to work as hard as when we're awake. If we don't get enough sleep or wake up often at night, we're at a greater risk of developing high blood pressure, coronary heart disease, obesity and stroke.

Sleep & weight

As we sleep, the levels of two hormones – leptin and ghrelin – change, which helps us maintain weight. Ghrelin increases appetite and it decreases with sleep. Leptin is associated with feeling full and it rises with sleep. However lack of sleep increases ghrelin and decreases leptin, leading us to eat more and gain weight, which in turn can lead to obesity and type 2 diabetes.

Sleep & metabolism

The circadian rhythms change the way our body handles certain hormones (see pages 22–4) and fat. They assist our liver, for example, to help in the digestion of fat at appropriate times. Inadequate sleep can lead to a decreased ability to produce insulin, an increase consumption of fatty, sweet and salty foods, and decreased physical activity, which can all lead to being overweight and obesity.

Sleep & immunity

Our body makes cytokines, a protein used to fight infection and inflammation. Without enough sleep, it becomes more difficult for our body to fight off infections.

Sleep & the amygdala

Activity increases in different parts of the brain during sleep. The amygdala, which is responsible for feelings of fear when in a stressful or threatening situation, can overreact when we don't get enough sleep, resulting in heightened responses and a depressed mood.

How much sleep do I need?

A number of factors affect how much sleep is needed, such as your age, genes and health. Someone who is recovering from an illness, injury or surgery will need more sleep, as will a woman in her first trimester of pregnancy. Here are general recommendations for daily hours of sleep based on age.

BIRTH TO 3 MONTHS OLD:
14–17 hours

4–12 MONTHS OLD:
12–16 hours (including naps)

1–5 YEARS OLD:
10–14 hours (including naps)

6–12 YEARS OLD:
9–12 hours

13–18 YEARS OLD:
8–10 hours

OVER 18 YEARS OLD:
7–9 hours

The body clock

Like every plant and animal, we have internal body clocks that synchronize our activities with the cycle of a 24-hour day. Our "circadian rhythms" respond to changes in environmental factors such as light and temperature (called zeitgebers). These responses are controlled by organs and glands around our body, which are, in turn, controlled by a biological clock in our brain.

As evening approaches and the sun sets, reduced levels of light trigger the brain to produce melatonin, a hormone that the body produces to help us sleep. Our core body temperature also drops, which makes us less alert. When exposure to light increases in the morning, our body stops producing melatonin and increases our core body temperature, making us more wakeful.

What do circadian rhythms do?

Circadian rhythms provide us with information to help us respond to the environment around us, helping us to conserve energy, find food, and grow and heal. They help regulate:

- **sleeping and waking**

- **core body temperature**

- **hormones**

- **metabolism**

- **immune system**

- **'flight and fight' response to stress**

- **our ability to think.**

"What hath night to do with sleep?"

John Milton, *Paradise Lost* (1667)

What causes misaligned circadian rhythms?

For refreshing, restorative sleep, we should align our sleep patterns with the natural cycle of daylight and darkness, but this doesn't always happen. Not going to bed when tired, disrupted sleep – from illness, stress, a noisy or bright environment, for example – or long naps during the day can disrupt our circadian rhythms.

Going against the natural rhythms

Travelling across multiple time zones can temporarily disrupt our circadian rhythms, causing jet lag until we get used to the light-dark cycle in our new location. Working shift patterns in which our work schedule, and therefore our sleep schedule, changes throughout the week can lead to us struggling to stay awake during our shifts at night-time and sleep in the daytime, leading to sleep deprivation.

What makes us sleepy in the daytime?

Having too much of a substance known as adenosine in our bloodstream might make us sleepy in the daytime. As we sleep, our body breaks down adenosine, but it builds up while we're awake and continues to until we're asleep again. If we haven't been getting enough sleep, this may explain why we need to take a nap.

The "wide awake" gene

Scientists have discovered a gene that seems to affect the timing of sleep. After they removed it from fruit flies, these flies struggled to fall and stay asleep. A fault in this gene might explain why some of us struggle to sleep, though other genes and lifestyle factors also have an impact.

Chronotypes

One way that scientists look at diurnal preference – our preferred times to be awake and asleep – is by chronotypes. Studies suggest that we inherit genes that determine if we are "early birds" who prefer to get up early or "night owls" who stay up late; sleeping when we're naturally inclined to sleep can improve our sleep quality and energy levels.

Based on a sleep-wake schedules, Dr Michael Breus has linked animals to these chronotypes:

Type	Lion
Wake up	6 am
Most productive	9 am–2 pm
Bedtime	10 pm
% of population	15% (aka early birds)

Type	Bear
Wake up	7 am
Most productive	10 am–2 pm
Bedtime	11 pm
% of population	55%

Type	Wolf
Wake up	7.30 am
Most productive	1 pm–5 pm
Bedtime	Midnight
% of population	15% (aka night owls)

Type	Dolphin
Wake up	6 am
Most productive	3 pm–7 pm
Bedtime	11 pm
% of population	10%

Different body clocks

Some people have circadian rhythms that don't follow a typical sleep-wake pattern. These include:

- **Advanced sleep-wake phase, where people feel sleepy, go to bed too early and wake up too early; they may have to force themselves to stay up late.**

- **Delayed sleep-wake phase, where people don't feel sleepy until very late at night; they often have a renewed burst of energy in the evening.**

- Non-24-hour sleep-wake rhythm disorder, in which someone's biological clock fails to connect with a 24-hour cycle; they find it difficult to maintain a typical sleep routine.

- Irregular sleep-wake rhythm disorder, in which someone's circadian rhythms do not control their sleep-wake patterns; they sleep in short intervals throughout the day.

Consequences of lack of sleep

Whether from a misalignment between our circadian rhythms and our environment or other reasons, not getting enough sleep can lead to fatigue and other mental and physical health problems. These include:

- Sleep problems that make it more difficult to fall asleep and stay asleep; this can lead to insomnia.

- Excessive sleepiness that can cause performance issues due to difficulty in focusing, remembering things and performing tasks.

- Sleep deprivation that makes it more difficult to regulate our emotions, leading to emotional, social and relationship problems as well as depression.

- Accidents and mistakes, including an increased risk of injury from handling tools or car accidents.

- Health problems such as obesity, type 2 diabetes, high blood pressure, heart attack and cancer.

Chapter Two

Sleep Cycles &
Deep Sleep

Sleeping in cycles

Based on our brain activity during sleep, there are two phases of sleep that repeat every 70–120 minutes, up to four to six cycles at a time. The two sleep phases are known as rapid eye movement (REM) sleep and non-REM sleep. There are three stages within non-REM sleep, making four distinct stages during a sleep cycle.

The Sleep Cycle

	Non-REM stage 1		Non-REM stage 2
1	5% DROWSY	2	45% LIGHT SLEEP
3	Non-REM stage 3	4	REM
	25% DEEP SLEEP		25% VIVID DREAMING

Non-REM stage 1

(also called N1)

This is a brief transition period between
wakefulness and sleep, marked by drowsiness.
During this stage, the heartbeat and breathing
begin to slow down. It lasts 1–7 minutes at
5% of our total sleep time and it is the
lightest sleep stage.

Non-REM stage 2

(also called N2)

In stage 2, the body temperature drops and
muscles relax. Eye movements stop and brain
wave patterns change. We spend 10–25 minutes
in stage 2 in the first cycle, but it increases
with each cycle – about 45% of our total
sleep time is in stage 2.

Hypnic jerks

In the nodding-off stage of non-REM stage 1 sleep, your muscle movements begin to diminish, although you may experience hypnic jerks, those sudden involuntary muscular twitches that may startle you awake. They can make you feel like you are falling, or be accompanied by flashing lights or crackling sounds.

Based on the word "hypnagogic", which describes the transition from wakefulness to sleep, these twitches often happen on one particular side of the body and appear to be completely random. According to the Sleep Foundation, they may be triggered by excess caffeine consumption, exercise before bedtime, stress and sleep deprivation. They happen to 70% of people.

Non-REM stage 3
(also called N3)

This is deep sleep, or slow-wave sleep. Long, slow waves known as delta waves produce electrical activity in the brain. In the first cycle, we spend 20–40 minutes in stage 3, but it gets shorter in the following cycles. About 20% of sleep is in this deepest non-REM sleep stage.

REM sleep

It is in REM sleep that our eyes move quickly, and our brain activity is the same as someone who is awake. We first get a few minutes of REM sleep after 90 minutes, but this stage gets longer, especially in the second half of the night. In adults, REM sleep accounts for 25% of our sleeping time.

Delta waves

High amplitude delta waves, or slow brain waves, characterize deep, dreamless sleep, but there are four other brain waves. Theta is a deeply relaxed, inward state; alpha is relaxed and passive; beta, the most common, is anxiety dominant with attention directed externally; and gamma is marked by concentrated focus and a highly active consciousness. Women have more delta-wave activity than men.

Delta waves are associated with another phenomenon, the K-complex, which immediately precedes delta waves in slow wave sleep. These short bursts of activity are thought to protect sleep while engaging in information processing.

Sleep paralysis

During REM sleep, we don't move our muscles except our eyes – which can be seen moving with the eyelids closed – and to breathe. This normal condition is known as atonia, which is the temporary paralysis of the muscles. Vivid dreaming occurs with atonia, and both typically end on waking, so you never become conscious of this inability to move.

However, if your consciousness does resume while you remain in paralysis, this is an abnormality of sleep and is likely to result in intense fear. You may have experienced this while in a state of semi-consciousness, in which you are trying to speak or move but you find you cannot. You may also feel a shortness of breath, chest pressure and emotions such as panic or helplessness during an episode. It is common to feel exhausted the next day.

Dream time

It is also during REM sleep that we have most of our vivid dreams, which may explain the brain activity although our muscles are paralysed (see opposite). Scientists believe that REM sleep is important for us to build our memories and for learning and creativity.

Sleep stages
Through the Night

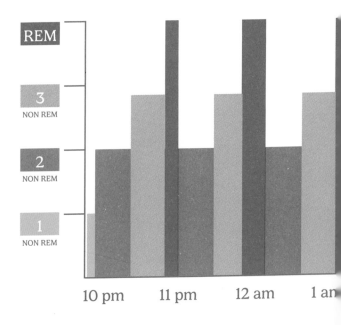

At first, during a night's sleep we spend more time in non-REM sleep, but by the second half of the night, we spend more time in REM sleep.

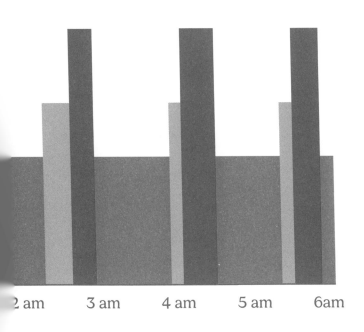

2 am   3 am   4 am   5 am   6am

Cycling through sleep

It's not only the amount of time in the stages that change. The amount of time of each sleep cycle is also different, progressing from shorter to longer cycles. The average length of the first cycle is 70–100 minutes, but by the final cycle, it can be 90–120 minutes long.

"Each night,
when I go to sleep,
I die.

And the next morning,
when I wake up,
I am reborn. "

Mahatma Gandhi, azquotes.com

How much deep sleep do you need?

When young, we need more deep sleep to promote development and growth. Perhaps because we're no longer growing, older people tend to get less deep sleep. In general, 25% of the time we sleep is in REM sleep, but only 13–23% of our total sleep is in deep sleep.

Newborns spend the most time in REM sleep, with deep sleep peaking in early childhood before sharply declining in teenagers. People under 30 years old tend to get 2 hours of deep sleep per night. If over 65 years old, we may get only 30 minutes of deep sleep.

> **Sleep is the golden chain that ties health and our bodies together.**

Thomas Dekker,
The Guls Horne-booke (1609)

Why is deep sleep important?

This is a deeply restorative sleep, when the brain can recover and rest. During deep sleep, the pituitary gland releases a hormone that helps regenerate cells and stimulates the body's tissues to grow. If we don't get adequate deep sleep, we'll feel sluggish rather than refreshed the next day; long term, it has health implications (see page 54).

Lack of deep sleep

Regular problems in getting deep sleep can lead to problems with our memory and retaining information. Long-term inadequate deep sleep has been linked to Alzheimer's disease, heart disease and other medical conditions.

Waking in deep sleep

During non-REM stage 1, any disruptions can easily wake someone up, since they are in a lighter sleep stage. However, if we try to wake someone up while in deep sleep, not only would it be much more difficult to arouse them, but once awake, that person would feel groggy for up to an hour afterwards.

A bad night's deep sleep

If we have a bad night's sleep that affects our quality of deep sleep, the next time we fall asleep, our body will try to compensate for this by going through the sleep cycles quickly to reach the deep sleep stage and stay there longer. Because most deep sleep happens in the first hour or so, sleep habits that help you fall asleep faster may also help you get more deep sleep naturally.

"**Having peace, happiness and healthiness is my definition of beauty. And you can't have any of that without sleep.**"

Beyoncé, Inc.com (March 2019)

Caffeine & deep sleep

Many of us drink coffee, tea and other caffeinated drinks to feel more awake. Caffeine achieves this by blocking adenosine, a chemical that induces sleep. Not only can drinking caffeine within 8 hours of our bedtime make it difficult to fall asleep, but it can also reduce the amount of deep sleep we get.

Alcohol & deep sleep

The sedative effect of alcohol can speed up sleep onset, so some sleepers enter deep sleep too quickly, leading to an imbalance of too little deep sleep and too much REM sleep, thereby affecting the overall quality of sleep.

Fragmented sleep

Older people often complain about interrupted sleep and having to get up to use the toilet. This may be because, as we age, less time is spent in deep sleep and more time in light sleep, so we're more easily aroused. Menopausal women may also have weakened circadian rhythms that impact their sleep-wake cycle.

Menopause

Women experiencing menopause may have disrupted sleep due to several symptoms:

- Night sweats caused by hot flushes.

- Insomnia, during and after the transition to menopause.

- Snoring and sleep apnoea (see page 62).

- Restless legs syndrome is experienced by more than 50% of post-menopausal women.

Sleep apnoea

A person who has sleep apnoea snores heavily and struggles to breath; this wakes them up, though it may be only briefly and they are unaware. They may have trouble falling asleep in the earlier stages of the first sleep cycle and fail to continue the cycle into deep sleep. They are often sleepy in the daytime.

Parasomnia

Unusual behaviours during sleep, known as parasomnias, occur in specific sleep stages. The person may make movements, noises or seem awake but not respond to people. Here are some of them.

- **NON-REM STAGES 1 AND 2:**
  SLEEP TWITCHES AND TEETH GRINDING

- **NON-REM STAGE 3:**
  SLEEPWALKING AND CONFUSIONAL AROUSALS (E.G. SUDDENLY SITTING UP BUT NOT AWAKE)

- **REM SLEEP:**
  NIGHTMARES AND HALLUCINATIONS

Exploding head syndrome

A parasomnia disorder, exploding head syndrome occurs when entering deep sleep or waking up in the middle of the night, in which a person believes they can hear the sound of an explosion, sometimes with flashes of light or muscle spasms. The noise isn't real; nevertheless, it causes distress that makes it difficult to fall asleep again.

"Gentle sleep, nature's soft nurse, how have I frighted thee, that thou no more wilt weigh my eyelids down, and steep my sense in forgetfulness?"

William Shakespeare,
Henry IV, Part II (c. 1597)

Nocturnal leg cramps

Sudden painful contractions of muscles at night-time in the lower legs – usually the calves – are painful and disrupt sleep, including deep sleep. They are more common in older people and in 73% of people they occur only at night.

Periodic limb movement disorder

Often confused with restless legs syndrome (feelings of itching, crawling and other unpleasant sensations when inactive), periodic limb movement disorder is when a person's legs make repetitive jerking or twitching movements while asleep. They can occur every 5–90 seconds for up to an hour and will cause fatigue the next day.

Chapter Three

Lifestyle Tips
for Deeper Sleep

Good sleep hygiene

There are three key practices that form part of what is known as good sleep hygiene.

- **Establishing a regular sleep schedule.**

- **Creating the right sleeping environment.**

- **Practising a healthy bedtime routine.**

But it doesn't end there: what we do in the daytime can affect our circadian rhythms and impact on our sleep.

Establish a wake-sleep pattern

To enjoy socializing, studying or working in our waking hours, we need to be well rested, which means a regular sleep routine. Decide on a wake-up time that is best suited to your situation, then calculate a bedtime based on that.

Don't sleep in

It is best to get up at the same time every day, whether a weekday or weekend. If you need to change your sleep schedule to wake up earlier or later, do so gradually, adjusting it by no more than an hour at a time.

Let there be light

Ensure you get plenty of exposure to sunlight by
opening curtains in the morning and spending
time outdoors. This will help your circadian
rhythms to establish that it is daytime and
release hormones so you stay more alert
when you should.

Try a sun alarm clock to simulate nature. It
combines a digital alarm with music and a light
to mimic a gradual sunrise and sunset.

"A well-spent day brings happy sleep.

Leonardo da Vinci, *The Notebooks of Leonardo da Vinci* (1888)

Get physical

Studies have found that exercise can reduce
the amount of time it takes to fall asleep,
improves sleep quality and reduces daytime
sleepiness. While intensive exercise within
3 hours of bedtime may be counterproductive
– it increases adrenaline levels, heart rate and
body temperature – less intensive exercise
between 4 pm and 8 pm may help people
fall asleep and improve deep sleep.

Time your exercise

Research indicates that to help improve sleep, these are the best times of the day for different exercises.

Morning
Try resistance exercise, such as lifting weights, or aerobic exercise, such as fast walking, to release melatonin earlier in the evening.

Afternoon
Now is the time for high-intensity exercise, such as running, for a better night's sleep without contributing to wakefulness.

Evening
Light resistance or aerobic exercise may lead to less waking in the night. Yoga, deep breathing and stretching can help ease you into sleep (see also pages 114–9).

Book dinner early

Avoid late-night meals, especially spicy or
heavy dishes, so there's time to digest them
before sleeping. If you need a snack closer
to bed time, choose those high in tryptophan
(see pages 100–101).

Don't smoke

There are many reasons not to smoke tobacco
products, but in regard to sleep, nicotine is a
stimulant and disrupts sleep.

Hack your diet

A diet low in carbohydrates, such as the ketogenic diet, has been shown increase the amount of delta activity and deep sleep in healthy individuals. Ketogenic diets have an effect on a brain chemical called adenosine, which builds up in the body during the day, decreasing wakefulness as the day goes on and promotes deeper slow-wave sleep at night. By stabilizing blood sugar levels, the diet can also help you avoid daytime sleepiness.

Avoid caffeine & alcohol

Imbibing on either of these in the evening hours will disrupt your circadian rhythm, reduce your sleep quality and keep you from getting replenishing REM and deep sleep.

According to the Sleep Foundation, moderate consumption of alcohol of more than 1 or 2 drinks will decrease your quality of sleep by 39%. Another study found that consuming caffeine 6 hours before bedtime reduced total sleep time by 1 hour. Caffeine can be found not only in coffee and tea, but energy drinks, energy bars, protein powders and chocolate.

> **"The waking have one common world, but the sleeping turn aside each into a world of his own. "**

Heraclitus, *Fragments* (c. 500 BCE)

> **When we feel like there isn't enough time in the day for us to get everything done, when we wish for more time, we don't actually need more time. We need more stillness.**

Christine Carter, *The Sweet Spot* (2015)

Dim the lights

Light can not only keep you stimulated but it has a negative impact on melatonin production, the hormone that tells us it's time to sleep.

- Dim room lights an hour before you head to bed.

- Make sure your curtains are drawn and use blackout curtains or blinds if your window has a sunny morning aspect.

- Turn off blue lights from electronic devices such as phones, tablets, TVs and laptops.

Practise
10-3-2-1-0

This is a great way to help you remember your pre-sleep health hygiene:

- Cut out caffeine 10 hours before bed.

- Don't eat food or drink alcohol 3 hours before bed.

- Stop working 2 hours before bed.

- Get away from your screens 2 hours before bed.

Groundhog night

Maintaining a regular schedule of going to bed and waking up at the same time each day can help us to fall asleep more easily and stay asleep. Before going to bed, follow the same ritual of brushing your teeth, changing into your nightclothes and whatever else you like to do.

End late-night toilet visits

One reason older people have interrupted sleep is due to needing to urinate in the middle of the night. Unless there's a medical reason behind this, making a few changes in your liquid consumption can mean an end to these late-night visits:

- Ban liquid consumption 3–4 hours before your bedtime (but ensure you stay well-hydrated during the day).

- Avoid drinks that can irritate your bladder. These include caffeine, which is also a diuretic (it increases the need to wee) and stimulates bladder activity, as well as alcohol and carbonated drinks.

- Double void. Empty your bladder before you brush your teeth and prepare for bed, then try again a second time.

Create calmness

Half an hour to an hour or so before bedtime, try an activity that will help you to wind down – the goal is to feel relaxed and calm. Some suggestions are:

- Take a warm bath (an hour before bed).

- Do some light stretching.

- Read a book.

- Listen to relaxing music.

Beds are for sleeping

With the exception of romantic interludes, it's best to restrict any activity in bed to sleep. This will help to establish in your mind that when you lie down in bed, you're there for nothing else other than sleep.

Choose
the best bedding

The quality and type of your bedding is a
personal choice but there are duvets and
bedlinen that help regulate your body
temperature and memory foam that adapts to
your body and posture. But you don't need the
latest technology; simply assess the season,
temperature of the room, whether you sleep
"hot" or "cold" and adjust the fabrics, weights
and layers accordingly.

Linens

The fabrics used for sheets, blankets, duvets and other bedding can make a difference to your comfort in bed. Natural materials, such as cotton and feathers, allow air circulation better than synthetics, so you're less likely to get sweaty in bed. In addition, sheets and pillowcases with a 200–400 thread count are less irritating for sensitive skin.

Throws & blankets

Layer your bed to anticipate different temperature needs during the night. A spare blanket at the foot of the bed or a textured quilt can easily be pulled up during the night.

Mattress & pillows

If your mattress or pillows are too hard, too soft or lumpy, they can make it difficult to fall asleep and may cause neck or back pain. It is well worth investing in new ones if the ones you have are no longer comfortable. Visit a shop to test before you buy.

Prepare the bedroom

You might be tired and have a comfortable bed, but what about the environment in the bedroom? To help improve your sleep quality, consider if you need to change or make any adjustments to your sleep environment. For example:

- Black-out curtains or heavy curtains will block out light (or wear an eye mask).

- Keep the room cooler (about 18°C/65°F).

- Wear ear plugs to block out noise, or use a fan or noise machine (see pages 122–3).

Love your PJs

Sleepwear should be comfortable and breathable for the best night's sleep, so choose nightwear in fabrics that feel soft and comfortable and – importantly! – fit well. Too small and you will feel constrained; too large and you may get twisted up in the fabric. You will never go wrong with silk, high-quality cotton, bamboo, linen, and in colder months, flannel. If you get cold feet, wear bedsocks that are loose, comfortable and lightweight.

Lavender aromatherapy

Many people find the scent of lavender oil can make them feel calm. It is an anxiolytic, which means it has a sedative effect that increases relaxation and calmness, and research has shown that it can increase deep sleep time. Never use lavender oil directly on the skin.

Just not sleepy

If you don't feel sleepy at your normal bedtime,
try a calming activity (see page 88) before going
to bed. If you've been in bed for about 20 minutes
and you still haven't fallen asleep, stress may be
keeping you awake. In this case, try a relaxation
technique or meditation (see pages 114–9).

Chapter Four

Sleep Solutions

A cup of tea

People have been drinking herbal teas for centuries as a natural sleep aid. The studies are limited, but some do indicate they may help us sleep. Try one of the teas opposite, but first check they won't interact with any medication you take.

Chamomile
The chemicals in this plant may promote a calming effect and modify the neurotransmitters involved in sleep.

Valerian root
The tea form may boost gamma-aminobutyric acid, a type of neurotransmitter, thereby reducing anxiety and improving sleep quality.

Low-caffeine green tea
This contains epigallocatechin 3-gallate, which can have a sedative effect.

Passionflower leaves
Either fresh or dried, these can be used to make a tea that may have a sedative effect.

Food to make you sleepy

While certain types of food can make it more difficult to fall asleep (see page 80), there are foods that can promote sleep.

Kiwis
Scientists aren't sure why, but studies indicate eating two kiwis an hour before bedtime can help you to fall asleep faster and have better quality sleep – it may be their high levels of serotonin or antioxidant properties.

Nuts
Walnuts, cashews, almonds and pistachios have a combination of magnesium, zinc and melatonin, which can help older adults with insomnia to sleep better.

Milk

Drink milk on its own and you'll get more melatonin, but combine it with a malted milk powder that contains vitamins B and D, and you may sleep through the night better.

Fatty fish

Eating salmon three times a week provides omega-3 fatty acids, needed to regulate serotonin, and has been shown in a study to improve overall sleep.

Tart cherries

Try drinking two glasses of tart cherry juice a day for better sleep quality and sleeping longer – the fruit has high levels of melatonin.

Turkey

The meat contains tryptophan, an amino acid that promotes good sleep and a good mood, according to research published in *Neuroscience & Biobehavioral Reviews*.

Cherry juice mocktail

According to Dr Charlene Gamaldo at Johns Hopkins Center for Sleep, tart cherry juice can improve your sleep. Social media influencers and users have jumped on this idea, combining it with magnesium and prebiotic soda for a "sleepy-girl" drink. Certainly cherry juice is rich in antioxidants, particularly a type called anthocyanins, and high in natural melatonin.

"The worst thing in the world is to try to sleep and not to."

F. Scott Fitzgerald, azquotes.com

Jet lag remedy

Travelling overseas? Get plenty of sleep 2–3 days beforehand. If travelling westwards, delay going to sleep by 20–30 minutes each day; if travelling eastwards, stay awake for an extra 10–15 minutes each day. At your destination, decrease light exposure at night and spend plenty of time outdoors in daylight. Short 10–15 minute naps are okay, but nothing longer.

On the night shift

If you have to work a night shift, try the following suggestions to help you sleep in the day:

- Ensure there are bright lights at your workplace.

- If drinking caffeine at work to stay alert, do so only at the beginning of a shift.

- Remove any sound and light distractions in your bedroom – consider wearing an eye mask.

Midnight anxiety

If you suffer from racing thoughts and a mind that won't rest at night, here are a few ways to turn off the noise in your head:

- **Journal your thoughts.** Physically writing them down gets them out of your head and somewhere else.

- **Listen to an app or podcast.** Choose one that specializes in sleep meditation or nature sounds.

- **Practise the 5-4-3-2-1 method.** Identify 5 things you can see, 4 you can touch, 3 you can hear, 2 you can smell and 1 you can taste. This technique anchors you to the present and diverts your thoughts.

Why nap?

Napping can have positive benefits such as reducing short-term fatigue and stress and improving mood, memory and energy, especially after a bad night's sleep. It can help improve workplace performance and improve logical reasoning and other cognitive functions. Naps can also support the immune system and lower the risk of cardiovascular problems such as heart attacks and stroke.

Naps are nothing new. The Spanish custom of having a siesta – of taking a long nap in the afternoon during the hottest part of the day – is well known. In Japan, it is customary to have *inemuri*, a short workplace nap.

Time your nap

The length of a nap is important. Because there isn't much time to go through the number of sleep cycles that we normally have when sleeping at night, a short nap of 20–30 minutes can be more restorative.

If a longer nap is necessary to counteract fatigue, a 90-minute nap allows time to go through a complete sleep cycle without interruption during deep sleep. By sleeping past the deep sleep stage, you should wake up feeling refreshed.

"Tired minds don't plan well. Sleep first, plan later."

Walter Reisch, azquotes.com

When to nap

To prevent a nap interfering with our regular bedtime, it's best to have a nap no closer than 8 hours before we normally go to sleep. For most of us, that means not having a nap after 3 pm. Fortunately, our circadian rhythms have a natural peak sleepy period in the early afternoon.

The best place to nap will be cool, quiet and dark
where there won't be interruptions. At home,
this is often a bedroom with blackout curtains.
Away from home, such as in an office setting, an
eye mask and earplugs may help.

Napping tips

- Have a caffeinated drink just before a short nap – we feel the peak effects of caffeine 30 minutes after consuming it, so you'll feel more alert when you wake up.

- Set an alarm for the length of time you wish to nap.

- When the alarm goes off, get up and do some stretching or walking to help wake up.

Napping No Nos

Napping isn't for everyone. For older people, napping during the day can lead to waking up often when sleeping at night, and regular naps over 60 minutes long have been linked to increasing the risk of type 2 diabetes.

Mindfulness & meditation

Stress and anxiety can often interfere with falling asleep. Meditation and mindfulness exercises to promote relaxation can improve sleep. You'll find some easy practices on the following pages, but you can join a group that teaches one of the following techniques:

- **Qigong, a type of traditional Chinese exercise that focuses on deep breathing combined with slow and quick movements.**

- **Tai chi, a form of Chinese martial art that consists of gentle movements following a form.**

- **Yoga, a combination of diaphragmatic breathing, mindfulness meditation and stretching in poses.**

- **Yoga nidra, a form of yoga that can induce a sleep-like state by focusing on chanting, breathing and awareness of different parts of the body.**

"Sleep and meditation are key. Natural sleep for 8 hours will help remove toxins from the body, help consolidate memory, create order from chaos. Sleep activates good hormones that are associated with rejuvenation and slowing down the ageing process."

Deepak Chopra,
Psychologies (April 2016)

Relax your muscles...

Struggling to fall asleep? Lie down, take a few deep breaths, then tense a group of muscles for 10–15 seconds, then relax them. Work from the bottom of the body to the top:

- Forehead, eyes and nose

- Mouth, cheeks and jaw

- Shoulders, arms and hands

- Tummy, back and buttocks

- Thighs and calves

- Feet and toes.

... Now relax your mind

Clearing your mind can help initiate sleep: soldiers in the US Army do this. After tensing and relaxing your muscles (see opposite):

- Imagine lying in a canoe in the middle of a calm lake, with blue skies above.

- Picture yourself in a dark room cuddled up in a black velvet hammock.

- Repeat a mantra such as "Don't think, don't think, don't think."

Breathe your way to sleep

With the lights off and in a quiet place without distractions, try this breathing meditation exercise to relax before bedtime.

1 Sitting in a chair or lying in bed, place one hand by your navel and the other on your chest.

2 Breathe in through your nose slowly, using your diaphragm, so the lower hand rises with your tummy but the hand on your chest doesn't.

3 Breathe out slowly. Repeat 10 times in controlled, calm breaths.

4 As you breathe in and out, clear your mind by focusing on your breathing. If you have a negative thought, acknowledge it, let it go and return to focusing on your breath.

"Sleep is
the best
meditation."

14th Dalai Lama, azquotes.com

Binaural beats

Listening to delta-wave frequencies of binaural beats, in which the right ear and left ear receive beats in a slightly different frequency, can increase the ability to fall asleep quicker and sustain longer deep sleep. You need to wear headphones to listen to binaural beat tracks, which are available online and on audio files.

White noise

The sound of white noise includes all audible frequencies. Researchers believe white noise masks background noises that can disrupt sleep. One study found listening to it helped adults fall asleep 38% faster. A fan or air purifier can be used as white noise, and white noise machines and apps are available.

Pink noise

The sounds of the ocean, a waterfall, rain or even birdsong played at night may help to increase deep sleep. These sounds, known as pink noise, are lower in pitch than white noise. They may be perceived as being calming and more suitable for some people than white noise.

Light therapy

Particularly in the shorter winter months, lack of light can disrupt the circadian rhythms, affecting sleep quality. Light therapy, which involves sitting in the morning by a special light box that emits high intensity light for 30–90 minutes, can help reduce melatonin and re-synchronize our body clock. Gradual sunrise alarm clocks may also be beneficial.

When all else fails...

Rule out medical problems: it's possible that
sleep apnoea (see page 62) or another medical
condition is responsible for your sleepiness.
If you feel sleepy all the time and have tried
following good sleep hygiene (see Chapter 3)
and the advice in this chapter, consider booking
an appointment with your doctor to rule out
a medical condition.

Medicines for sleep

Researchers are looking for breakthroughs, but for now your doctor might prescribe a medicine only if a sleep problem is severe. The limited options all have side-effects, and can lead to drowsiness that causes accidents. Options include:

- **Benzodiazepines and Z-drugs,** which are addictive so are only suitable short term.

- **Tricyclic antidepressants such as trazodone,** which seem to interact with histamines (compounds released in an allergic reaction) and may increase deep sleep.

- **Antihistamines,** which are available over the counter, but they can cause insomnia if used long term.

- **Melatonin** to over 55-year-olds, but only for up to 10 weeks.

- **Sleep patches** are imbued with melatonin, lavender, 5-HTP, CBD and natural oils like lavender, valerian or magnesium, or combinations of these.

There is a time for many words, and there is also a time for sleep.

Homer, *Odyssey* (c. 700 BCE)